Waste Less Time, Gain More Customers

Angel Tuccy
Eric Reamer

Copyright © 2012

Waste Less Time, Gain More Customers

Angel Tuccy & Eric Reamer

Website: www.ExperiencePros.com
Blog: www.ExperienceProsBlog.com
Twitter @ExperiencePros
Facebook: Facebook.com/ExperiencePros
Mobile App on iPhone & Android: Experience Pros Radio

ISBN-10: 1479245003

ISBN-13/EAN-13: 978-1479245000

BISAC: New Business Enterprises, Small Business & Entrepreneur

5-step approach to helping small business thrive into a multi-million dollar enterprise.

Bonus Chapter Excerpt from *Lists That Saved My Business*.

All Rights Reserved.

*Waste Less Time,
Gain More Customers*

"The business plan included everything I needed to start and grow my business, except for one thing. Customers."

Table of Contents

Chapter 1	Quit Wasting Time	11
Chapter 2	Write It Down	17
Chapter 3	The 80/20 Rule	37
Chapter 4	Visibility Cloak	51
Chapter 5	Make The Sale	67
Chapter 6	Retain Your Customers	79
Excerpt	Lists That Saved My Business	99

As an entrepreneur, you get to work half days:
7am until 7pm.
You get a day off every week.
It's called Sunday.
You get to create a legacy,
out of your garage.
The dreams that excite you,
scare most people.
When you take a call on your vacation, it isn't
work, because you love what you do.
When you love what you do,
you never work a day in your life.

Chapter 1
Quit Wasting Time

I've often thought about writing the world's shortest book on weight loss and one on financial freedom. The book on weight loss would have three chapters: Eat Better, Eat Less, and Exercise More. The book of financial freedom would have two chapters: Spend Less, Save More. Each book would be straight to the point, no messing around. There are days when that's exactly how I want to barrel through. No fluff, just get the work done.

And then, there are the other days. Distractions, both fun and annoying, are far more interesting. The television, people, Facebook, Twitter, hanging out at the coffee shop, all seem like a better idea, even if I know there's work to be done or tasks to be finished, and phone calls to be made.

The two largest categories of books are for weight loss and financial improvement. Even with all the information in world, these topics continue to plague our society. You know your weight doesn't define you. The balance in your bank account doesn't define you, though there are days when it feels like it. It's the choices you make every day, healthy or unhealthy, that get in your head and given enough time, they set up permanently. When you repeat these choices frequently enough, new habits, good or bad, are taught.

The concepts around self-help and self-improvement aren't rocket science, though there's a lot of science behind living healthier lives and algorithms for compound interest.

The extra chapters in all those books get to deal with the stuff we load into our heads everyday.

I know that it's not as simple as writing two or three chapters. Nothing ever is. Life's complicated. Life is demanding. Life is too short to waste your time. You have things to do, places to go and people to see. Yet, everybody else wants a piece of your time, too. They feel entitled to be given a chunk. And when you give them a little bit, they want more.

You have well-meaning people in your life who distract you all the time, causing you to make tough decisions against what you *want* to do versus what you *need* to do. Especially when you add in the challenging category of what you think you *should* do. There are complete strangers who derail your focus, along with the mass media constantly grabbing for your attention.

Weight loss and financial planning have so many variables for how the end result could look like. Each individual has a different height and weight; your ideal body composition is unique to you. When it comes to financial success, the amount of money you want to have in your bank account varies from person to person.

Your head is filled with three competing thoughts all the time: What do I want? What do I need? What do I think it should be?

When it comes to spending time, each and every person on the planet has the same 24 hours to spend in a given day. There are no rollovers, like with your cellphone plan or PTO (paid time off) days. Each day, the clock ticks for everyone.

There are people who cram so much into a 24-hour time frame that it makes my head spin. There are people around me who have been telling me for months about what they "plan" to do, yet it never quite makes it to their "I got it done" list.

What makes one person so adept at accomplishing more than every one else around? How do they figure you what needs to be done, and actually manage to fulfill it?

The difference is planning.

People who succeed don't get there by accident. They plan for success, and they don't mess around. It doesn't mean that they're work-a-holics and never take time for fun. They work hard and they play hard.

When they write down their goals, it's not a one-time, write-it-down-stick-it-in-a-drawer-and-hope-it-comes-true type of success plan. It's a working, living, breathing document.

WANT | NEED | SHOULD

Chapter 2
Write It Down

I admit, for 25 years, I carried around my Franklin planner and devoted time each and every day planning out my days, week, months, and yes, even years. Nothing happened until I first put it in the calendar. I used my calendar as a journal, goal setting and to ensure that my checklists got checked off. I made checklists and the most important items on the list ended up on my calendar with a time and date to accomplish them. I never left home without my planner. It was as much a part of my outfit as my shoes. Every few years, I'd update the binder and give my planner a new style. Every October, I'd be as excited as a child at Christmas time when I'd head into the store to purchase next year's refill.

I'd read magazine articles on time-management and I'm a sucker for any title that starts with a checklist of "5 Ways to …" I love being organized and ready for the events of the day.

I am surprised by the behavior of dear friends of mine who don't write anything down. I'm amazed that they don't consult a calendar and yet manage to keep their appointments.

I am further surprised at how often I meet someone who doesn't have a single goal written down. With everything that we know about the habits of highly successful people, why in the world aren't people writing down their goals?

Being spontaneous and creative have their place in experiencing the joy of life. Waking up in the morning and going where the wind blows you sounds so romantic and exotic.

Traveling to distant places with only your backpack and a compass make for great stories and a lifetime of memories. Having a lifestyle where people aren't depending on you to bring home a regular paycheck is pretty foreign to the circles I travel in.

For small business owners, entrepreneurs, network marketers and commission-sales people, your livelihood requires that your hours aren't wasted, but in fact, are spent bringing more customers through your sales process. But do you know how many more? Without a written goal of what you need to accomplish, the chances of hitting your mark is fairly inconsistent, to be polite.

Write down this phrase: I own a multi-million dollar enterprise. Say it out loud. Saying it out loud should make your toes tingle. Your business is going to produce serious revenue. You're not running a hobby anymore.

You have a multi-million dollar company sitting at your fingertips, even if the bank deposit doesn't reflect it, yet. YET. Mind you, it's not about the money, it rarely is. It's about your mindset. Whether or not the dollars are important to you, you need to treat your company, and your time, as if you're running a thriving enterprise. Otherwise, well-meaning friends, television and Angry Birds will distract you.

You'll put off making phone calls or setting appointments if you don't have the mindset to take your business seriously. If you work at home, you'll stay in your slippers far too long and then decide that you've stayed home this long, you might as well wait until tomorrow to get anything finished.

As I write this chapter, the end of the month just passed and I've turned the page, though now virtually, over to the new month.

Yes, I made the switch from carrying a Franklin Planner to using an app on my smartphone. Though, the jury is still out about how effective virtual calendaring will be for me.

While I can translate the calendar portion of my Franklin to a virtual app that syncs to my phone, laptop and any other device of my choosing, it's deeply lacking in other features.

I enjoy the fact that I don't have to carry around the binder anymore, and my phone encases my annual agenda. I can add events and meetings easily, and even include directions, location, add who else will be there and lots of nifty features including color-coordinating with other agendas. I can quickly duplicate, delete or reschedule without the need of whiteout tape or the distraction of the mess that comes when I cross out an appointment. In order to work within the small grid, I had perfected writing in a microscopic-size font that only I could decipher.

However, I've now had to download a note-taking app, an app for contacts, another for writing down my goals and one for keeping checklists. I now carry around a small notepad for general note taking. But I've embraced technology, I'm told.

The biggest difference between these two months (last month versus next month) is drastic.

Last month could go on record as being a banner month for many people in business. I'm celebrating the fact that I hit all of my sales goals. Many in my sphere have also seen their sales increase by record numbers over the previous year. One could say that their marketing efforts have finally kicked in and the results of months of hard work are finally paying off. They would be right.

But there was also a strong force of nature on their side that can't be discounted.

For my calendar-loving friends, who set up sales goals and track them throughout the month, even down to the day, you may already know where I'm going with this.

Last month (which happened to be August) had 23 working days, whereas, September will only have 19 working days. It's as if you were given an entire extra workweek to run your multi-million dollar enterprise. Bonus!

For all those time when you've muttered to yourself, I just wish I had more time; Mother Nature gifted you the month of August. And it usually happens twice a year. We can all get tons accomplished when there's more time.

The secret to time management is surviving the months in between with only 19 working days.

If you know your sales quota for each day, you'll know that it changes each month, ever so slightly. Going from a month of 23 working days into a month of 19 working days, there's no time to delay or goof off. It's time to get down to business and ensure that you've got a time-management plan to get you through the end of month and make payroll. You are running a multi-million dollar company.

Now you're thinking that you definitely need more customers. Let me tell you this. You don't need MORE customers.

You're thinking, "Yes, I do".

I hear it all the time, "I need more customers".

Okay, how many more? The answer can't just be MORE. How will you measure MORE? Is one more customer enough? Is it 10% more? 20%? Write down your real goal.

How many do you have now? Probably more than you know. Is every person in your database a current customer? Do you know how often they shop with you?

The key to hitting a goal is having a goal.

Before you begin the new month, you have to know what you want it to look like at the end of the month. It's your roadmap. It's your guide. It's your measurement against how close or far you are from getting there.

It's also your motivation.

When you see that you're 75% closer, your adrenaline kicks in. Your energy increases. You're focused. You're determined. You know you can do it. You've seen what it takes to get this far and you can duplicate it.

In October 2008, an associate suggested that we start a radio program. Recording audio programs and podcasting them on the Internet was beginning to trend and anyone with a cellphone and an Internet connection was becoming the host of their own radio show.

Internet radio was the new "brochure" for your business. Much like writing a book is now a gateway or business card for your company, that's how podcasting Internet shows were being promoted back then.

I say back then, as if four years ago was so significant, but the Internet changes everything so lightning fast. We were fortunate to be in that wave.

Nine months after starting our podcast show, we switched from Internet to (what they call) terrestrial radio. This is what you have in your car. You can listen to our show on your AM dial. For the most part, our business model stayed the same. We continued to offer business training and business consulting, while hosting a 30-minute daily talk show on the AM dial.

We set new business goals, and having a radio presence increased our credibility. You could tune in and listen to us every single day and the message was the same as our business training. During the next 15-months, our business steadily increased, and we were able to publish a couple of books. Even though the business model was stable, a significant shift was taking place. We began to dream bigger.

The most significant change wasn't what our business model was doing; it was our dream for what our business model could be. From the very first day of broadcasting on the AM dial, a dream was triggered.

My background wasn't public speaking. I was never on the main stage like my co-host, Eric. Eric traveled the globe entertaining and teaching for fifteen years before I met him. He can stand in front of a crowd and speak clearly into a microphone and never struggle. He has the gift and the talent. It doesn't hurt that he's 6 foot 5 and has a strong, smooth voice.

Eric took me under his wing and helped me to become a public speaker. He took me in quivering and shaking, with my butterflies no where near flying in formation, and introduced me to the world I am now deeply in love with. *They* say the best way to get over a fear is to face it and that's what happened to me.

In those early days, I was a trembling, nervous wreck whenever I stood in front of an audience. I had no idea that I could hold on a conversation or speak to a group about a helpful topic. Fast forward the clock and I'm on the public radio every single day, and regularly speak in front of crowds ranging from small classrooms to large conferences.

The first day on the air imparted a brand new goal that had never existed before. The new goal for both of us was immediately born to become nationally syndicated radio hosts of a 3-hour daily program. Granted, that's a long ways away from the starting point of being a 30-minute program on one station. That's the beauty of it. It doesn't matter where you're starting from, your starting point will be the impetus for inspiration. The greatest success stories are filled with failure and humble starting points in life. Take heart and know the worse off you are, the better your story will be. You have nowhere to go but up and the only thing standing between you and success is if you think you can't do it. Of course you can do it.

Of course you can do it. Believe in yourself. And when you feel like you can't, surround yourself with those that believe in you more than you believe in yourself until you get to the place where you can say out loud, "Of course I can do it."

Goal Setting is the Simple Act of Writing Down What You'd Like To Do

Simple goal-setting starts with writing down things you'd like to do, places you'd like to see and whatever is on your mind that you haven't accomplished. Take however much time you need. This isn't the sort of exercise you accomplish in one sitting. This is a forever and on-going list. Each day will bring new ideas and new adventures to your mind. Keep a running tab on all of them. Make sure you add, "Turn my company into a multi-million dollar enterprise" to the list. Remember, it's not as much about the money as it is about creating the mindset that you are the CEO of a thriving company.

Writing down personal goals is the hardest part of all of this. Too often, adults have lost the ability to dream big. I mean really dream big. The *"nothing is impossible"* big stuff. The downside to growing up is the realization that comes with dreaming. You know that each goal requires money and maybe talent and all the other excuses that never got in the way when you were a child and you thought you really could be Batman®. The easy route is to stop dreaming, and that's what most people do.

The people who hit top sales goals, who accomplish the most in a given 24-hour day, are those who dream big. Breathe some life into those dreams again. Put yourself back on the path that says, "I can do this".

Time Frame | Action Steps | Deadline

For your sales goals, take each individual goal and assign a time frame, deadline and the action steps to make it happen.

Input the action steps into your calendar. I am most productive in hitting sales goals when I start my week with sales appointments already set. This week, even if I'm busy, I am setting appointments for next week. This keeps me from riding the sales process rollercoaster.

When I look at my calendar and see the multiple meetings that bring in revenue are already set in my calendar, I know it's going to be a productive week.

I start the week on a high note and even if some of those meetings get rescheduled, or one or two don't go as planned, I know that that I have several others keeping me motivated.

You have goals to meet each and every day, or maybe in your line of work, your goals are weekly. The process is still the same, no matter what your deadline is.

When your goals are written down, and your action steps are in your calendar, you can let the time-wasters stop gaining traction. Each minute, the clock is ticking. When you're at work, each minute is precious and the time it takes you hit your goals is finite. You don't have an eternity. In fact, you don't have the luxury of putting off until tomorrow what you can do today. The lie we all tell ourselves is that there's always more time and it's okay to delay. That's not true. Today is all you truly have. The thing is, you know what you need to do. You know when you need to do it. Stop wasting precious time and get to it. Of course you can do it.

In general, the worse case scenarios only happen in your head. You are your worst critic and the biggest procrastinator and there's no good reason for it. You have a calendar. You have the goals for success written down. You have deadlines. Don't play small. Go out and grab that dream for yourself. No one else will. No one else will make your dreams a priority.

The Cheshire Cat in *Alice In Wonderland* told Alice that as long as she didn't care where she was going, it didn't matter which route she took. The same philosophy is true with your plans. If you don't have any action steps or deadlines, then you won't be able to track and measure growth. You won't realize just how close you are, or how far off track you really are.

Set The Bar Higher

My friend Ron wanted to help raise money for charity. He set forth a challenge to help raise funds, but rather than say he was raising money, he put an actual figure to the challenge. His challenge was to raise $1,000.00 for this fundraiser.

By establishing a clear dollar amount, everything raised was measured against the goal. As the donations increased, it was easy to share how close he was and motivation increased when they celebrated milestones along the way. You can rally the troops to keep going once they've hit the halfway mark. Others will step up to help when they see that you're close to accomplishing the target.

If Ron would've said, "I'd like to raise some money for this charity," he could have been satisfied when they raised $400.00. With four hundred dollars already earned, where is the incentive to keep going? When you set a goal to chase an unknown factor, the end-result causes you, and others around you to feel let down. You know you can do more, but without having a clear incentive, you allow the unknown factor to cause more damage than good.

By clearly setting the marker, you keep the motivation and measuring progress is built in.

Can you overshoot and blow your goals out of the water by totally exceeding them? You bet you can! The key is to continue to set a new goal along the way. If you hit your $1,000 charity goal early on, you can increase the goal to by 50%. If you hit that with enough time before the deadline, you can increase it again by 50%. You're never working against an unknown factor.

Set your business goals. Write them down. Give them a deadline and work the action steps to accomplish them.

Believe That Anything Is Possible

When we taught Experience Pros University, each student took an oath of commitment that carried him or her past the initial excitement phase, when work really starts to feel like work and you want you to go back to your old habits.

> *No Excuses*
> *Believe That Nothing Is Impossible*
> *Commit to Showing Up*

In your business, writing down your goals is the first step to committing to them.

Eliminate any excuses, and surround yourself with people that believe in you.

Time Frame | Action Steps | Deadline

Chapter 3
The 80/20 Rule

Not every person you interact with is a potential client. The truth is, sales in not a numbers game and every *"no"* does not lead you closer to a *"yes"*. Who was the brainchild behind the messaging that fed us that line of bologna? The world of bringing in new clients and increasing revenue is a tough one. There are a hundred things you would rather do than pick up the phone and ask one more stranger if this is a good time for them. Knocking on strangers doors and making unsolicited phone calls is a terrible job, admittedly by anyone who's ever had to bring back a stack of business cards to their manager or dial for dollars off a list that was found in some archaic database.

One of the students who took our course *"How To Gain and Retain More Customers"* later wrote us a testimonial. He said, "Eric and Angel saved my sole." He was referring to the sole of his shoe. He used to wear out a pair of shoes every six months.

His job as the salesperson for his company was to knock on doors. He would go door-to-door soliciting his service. He was given a geographic area that his company was targeting and hit the pavement. He was a pro. He enjoyed his job and he felt like he was good at it. He would wear out the sole of his shoes by putting in so many miles.

When we looked at the sales numbers and identified where new business came from, it was determined that 20% of all new business came from these solicitations. Consider your own business, 20% growth is a number to be proud of. When we put together a list of terms that described their ideal customer, geography never came into the discussion.

For some, geography is a major descriptor, but one size does not fit all. A zip code is not always the most effective way to put together an Ideal Customer list.

When this company looked at who their best customers were, the types of product they manufactured, became the number one trait. Once they identified this trait, it made it far easier to market to only their ideal customer and stop wasting time knocking on doors of non-ideal customers. Scott could stop replacing his shoes, and he was grateful to us for saving his sole.

Take a look at your favorite customers. Your favorites are the customers who don't feel like work. You enjoy their phone calls, rather than dread having to talk to them. They pay on time, rather than having to be repeatedly invoiced. They're regular clients, and a simple reminder from you is welcomed. They love your product and you don't have to convince them of the benefits. They think your pricing is fair and aren't constantly complaining or comparing you to the cheaper competition. They play an active role in the conversation and aren't defensive when you suggest an idea. They get excited when you bring out something new, rather than make excuses not to see you. It's a relationship, not a transaction.

There are favorite clients and there are clients you would like to fire. Chances are, if you're feeling strained about doing business with your customer; they're feeling the same way. If a little communication can't remedy the situation, chances are, they aren't your ideal customers, and more than likely, you must refer them to someone else.

It's not worth your time to chase around prospects that aren't your ideal customer. If they give you grief on the front end, you'll end up being further grieved down the road. I received a great piece of advice one day when I was told to "fight my battles on the front end". The logic here is that you won't delay the battle with a customer if it's not the right fit. You can either discover it now, when it's easiest to break free, or later, when feelings get hurt and leave everyone feeling raw from the experience.

It's a bird, it's a plane, it's Super Busy! When it comes to getting things done, we're all Super Heroes.

These days, your prospects are Super Busy. There isn't anyone who isn't, so calling you back, making their next order or in general, staying in touch with you, isn't their biggest priority. They are busy building their own business; so don't jump to the conclusion that, just because they haven't called you back, they're not interested. They're probably really interested but they need you to be persistent. In other words, it's up to you to do your job.

> *"The rock wasn't cut in half because the water was powerful. The rock was cut in half because the water was persistent."*

Your ability to bring more customers through your sales process is equal to the amount your customers trust you. They trust you to sell them only products they need. This means, *you will only sell your product to a customer that needs your product*. This is your ideal client. Not every one who can fog a mirror needs your product.

To put this in perspective, I'll demonstrate with two run-of-the-mill industries, a Chiropractor and a Plumber. Much like you, they have a lot of competition and don't really feel like they have something that sets them apart. Both feel like everyone in the country is their ideal customer because everyone has a spine and everyone has a toilet. So as they begin to build a website, create a social media presence and determine where to advertise, they run into a big dilemma. They don't know who benefits the most from their service. Men or women, young or old, white collar or blue collar, city or suburbia, family or single, coffee or tea? According to each business owner, it's every one. There's no way to build a marketing plan that caters to Every One.

Everyone needs my product.
It's perfect for everyone.
Everyone, everyone.
But I can't describe them for you.

The excuse for not identifying an ideal client is the fear that you will turn business away, and right now, you need every client you can get.

When we started Experience Pros, our answer to "who is our ideal client?" used to be "anybody who will pay me." Another terrible reply is "our ideal client is small to medium-sized companies". That describes no one, ever. I'm betting that not only does it NOT describe an ideal client; it also makes the describer sound desperate and unprofessional.

You need a certain number of more clients and you need to stop wasting your time getting them. What sets you apart from your competition and ensures that you're not wasting your marketing resources is to identify and market to your ideal client. I want your ideal client to be as unique as possible.

I read about a real estate agent who was kicking her competition in the teeth in a declining real estate market. Everyone around was in dire straights for keeping their doors open, except for this one woman. She catered to a unique clientele.

A Very Unique Clientele

See if you can picture this. She describes her ideal client as a Harley-Davidson®-motorcycle-riding Polish Woman. Now, it doesn't get any clearer than that. You can absolutely create an image in your mind of this woman. It might describe someone you already know or have met. If you ever come across a woman on a hot rod motorcycle with a thick European accent that happens to be in the market for a new home, you would instantly be able to offer her an ideal recommendation. There's only one woman in the world that would get your referral. She also sells homes for the friends of these women because her service fits a lot of demographics, but her ideal client is her sweet spot and it's where 80% of her business comes from.

That's excellent branding. That's creating word-of-mouth marketing. And that's a success story you can duplicate.

Just because you think everyone can use your product, doesn't mean you should sell it to him or her.

Now, back to our chiropractor friend. He specializes in treating competitive bike racers. Do you know any competitive bike racers? If you meet one who is complaining about his back or achy joints, you know who to refer him to. He advertises on sports shows, in bike shops and in local cycling magazines. He always has a booth at the bike races. He also treats people who don't even own a bike. He treats family members of the bike racers. He treats a lot of people because his service fits a lot of different lifestyles, but his sweet spot is competitive bike racers and that's where 80% of his business comes from.

The plumber created a similar success story.

He specializes in treating homes for root damage in a specialized part of town where the homes were built during the turn-of-the-century and the hundred-year old trees have an established root system that wreaks havoc on the plumbing.

He puts flyers on the doors in this neighborhood, he places yard signs when he's providing a service and he keeps an extra truck strategically parked nearby, where traffic and visibility in and out of the neighborhood is high. The truck has a vehicle wrap that has a specially branded phone number just for this neighborhood.

He advertises in the local coupon book that targets this neighborhood and has a website that includes this neighborhood in the SEO package (Search Engine Optimization, making sure he gets found by the most popular key words people are searching for). He does business in other neighborhoods, too, but his sweet spot has a zip code that brings him 80% of his business.

Don't be afraid to clearly identify your ideal client. It will clear up so much confusion for you and for your referring clients. They'll be able to clearly identify great prospects for you. You'll know exactly where to market yourself. You'll be able to create a website that clearly speaks to your prospects hot buttons.

When we're on the air, we've developed a sweet spot for speaking to business owners and entrepreneurs. Every now and then, we get off track and bring in a topic that doesn't perfectly fit. This is when our producer comes to us and reminds us that we have a sweet spot that our listeners depend on.

One of the easiest things to do is stop listening and push the button for a new channel. When we stay on-topic, we speak directly to our ideal clients, in this case, our listeners.

We have an added obligation of keeping our ideal clients listening because our sponsors are counting on us. They are putting their advertising on our show with the goal of speaking to business owners and entrepreneurs. We can't afford to waste time and speak to topics that retirees or stay-at-home spouses are looking for. We have all demographics listening, but more than 80% of our audience fills our unique niche.

Once you identify your ideal client, you have the ability to filter out the non-ideal clients. This is valuable information. Too often, your time is spent chasing down prospects that will never buy from you. You waste time trying to convince someone that your product is right for him or her. Even if you make the sale, your time and resources are wasted because they took up too much time and most likely won't ever shop with you again because they're not ideal.

This happens a lot when you first open your proverbial doors and you're selling to friends and family. The immediate success is gratifying, but eventually, you need to stop hitting up mom and neighbors and build your multi-million dollar enterprise from a pipeline of ideal clients.

You need to do business with people who like you, trust you and want to refer others to you. Your time is too valuable to just be busy. Busy doesn't pay the bills. Busy doesn't help you reach your goals. Busy, busy, busy doesn't cut it. You need to be productive.

Focus on the right prospects. Put your energy and resources into building a website, business card and packaging that speaks directly to the emotions of your clients, rather than the logics.

Become their favorite and they'll become loyal, braggin' fans.

I specialize in...

My Ideal Client Traits

*People do business with people they know, like, and trust.
In other words,
people *do business with* people.*

Chapter 4
Wear Your Visibility Cloak

Location, location, location. It's the secret sauce to real estate. It's also your secret weapon to building customer relationships. You want to be everywhere your customers are. Think of your brand as Visa®, it's everywhere you want to be. Take lessons and ride on the research of big brands to grow your company. They have an advantage of a large sales force and significant marketing budgets. You too, have a marketing advantage. You have looked every single one of your customers in the eye and shaken their hand. You know them. You have a relationship with them.

The tendency for small business owners is to underestimate that power. Small is only a state of mind. You can be everywhere your customer is, once you start thinking like Visa®.

Big brands have done the research for you and most of it can be found by doing a little homework yourself either at the library, Small Business Development Centers or on the Internet. I found that Coca-Cola® wants you to see their brand 358 times per day. Per day! Now compare that to your plan of sending out a newsletter once a month. How in the world do you expect to keep up and grow your company with 12 impressions a year, compared to bigger brands vying for the same dollars from your customer? You can't. There's absolutely no comparison.

In advertising, most radio stations will encourage you to invest in a 100-commercial package. The reason is because there are hundreds of other messages targeting your same audience and you need to infiltrate. More, more, more. This is especially important if you're brand new. If no one has heard of you before, you are starting at ground zero to build a reputation for yourself.

Your brand needs to communicate a promise of trust and credibility. The way the brain works, you need to see something twelve times before you begin to remember that you've ever seen it at all. Once you hit the tipping point, is when you start to build on the trust and eventually, that trust turns into business.

Contrast that formula with meeting someone for the first time at a networking event and he or she immediately assumes you'll want to do business with him or her. Fail. Unless I've heard of you before, I won't immediately part with my money, change where I'm currently shopping, and trust you to take care of my needs. Even if I'm completely disgruntled with my current provider, I'm more likely to stay where I'm familiar before switching to some unknown company. Contrary to what customers will tell you, they aren't looking for better, they're looking for familiar. You can be that familiar brand by building a strategic presence.

Channels 1, 2, 3, 4, 5, 6, 7, 8, 9, & 10

Be the Visa® for your brand. Choose ten marketing channels. Most can be free or very low cost. In fact the first seven channels can be activities that only require your time and not your money. Think of networking, social media, blogging, optimizing your key words on search engines and using Google® +, sitting on a board of directors or volunteering for committees, writing articles, and speaking for trade groups. While setting up your marketing channels, keep your branding consistent by matching up all your promotional materials, and having quality promotional products. Never print your own business cards.

A brand new retailer held an open house and invited the local chamber of commerce group. Her clothing store catered to women, so inviting the local women's business groups was targeting her ideal clients.

It was brilliant to host an event, invite her ideal clients and showcase her wares.

There were refreshments and prizes. The only thing missing was sales weren't being encouraged. More than that, she let the group know that because she is new, she doesn't have a budget for marketing so she's heavily relying on her customers for word-of-mouth referrals. Seriously? Yes, it's important to let your clients know you appreciate their referrals, and they have the ability to outdo your sales force, once you have a system in place, but is it a smart business plan to hand off the bulk of your marketing to someone who doesn't have an invested interest? If you're struggling and you expect your customers to do what you're not willing to do, you will become an IRS statistic.

Another gal just opened up a fitness center. Because she is functioning on a minimal budget, she is in the store all day long running low-attended classes and working on paperwork so she can't be out marketing to bring in new clients.

They both ask the same question, "What can I do for free to bring in more clients? I opened up a store, but where do new customers come from?" It's the same question we all find ourselves asking at some point or another. We especially start finding ourselves asking this question when the economy shifts. What worked before doesn't seem to be working anymore. Or what I thought would work, never seemed to really take off.

My friend was into playing an Internet game called FarmVille®. He was so engaged in the game and wanted me to know how much playing FarmVille® helped him understand business. He explained to me that the principles of the game were very similar to real-life business practices. In the game, you have to plant seed, harvest your crops, take the crops to the market to sell, and reinvest your money for new seed.

Not to be a wet blanket on his enthusiasm, the business coach in me came out to play.

I wanted to learn more about the marketplace process of the game. In the game, how do the customers know about the marketplace? How do the customers know when the marketplace is open and what vendors will be there? How do the customers choose your booth versus a competitor's booth?

As a participant of the game, your role was to be the farmer. There was no active role in marketing other than showing up at the market with your basket of goods and the customers showed up, bought everything you had, and at the end of the day, your bank account was full.

I was very frustrated at the concept that the game was teaching that if you have something to sell, customers will show up to buy it. That's what gets entrepreneurs into trouble. Entrepreneurs often mistakenly assume the customers will just show up. But what if they don't?

The Internet offers so many free marketing resources that entrepreneurs undervalue the effort, and therefore, underestimate their own value.

You have to be strategic in keeping your brand in front of your customers, pretty much 24 hours a day. You have to give them a reason to return your phone calls and engage you in an easy conversation that's a win-win for everyone. You need them to refer you, but the only strategy you know is to do a great job and HOPE they refer you.

Without customers, you don't have a multi-million dollar enterprise; you have a hobby. When you search around for free PR and cheap ways to market your company, you undermine your own mindset. Most entrepreneurs keep to the free or low cost marketing for far too long. Their mindset keeps them thinking too small.

You are a multi-million dollar enterprise. Imagine you're about to be endorsed by a major brand. They like your company, they believe in you and they want to endorse you.

This happened to my friend, Mary.

Mary was so excited that a major celebrity was endorsing her brand new company. She immediately came up with a marketing strategy to promote the endorsement. This was no time to play small, but to represent her company in a big way.

The thing you need to keep in mind is this: you don't need a celebrity endorsement to get started. You can create all that marketing buzz and PR for yourself, from right where you are. You don't have to wait to be "discovered" to create a fantastic PR campaign.

Each quarter, we put together a campaign that uses ten marketing channels. It gives us a reason to put our brand in front of our customers and keep our brand on the tip of their tongue.

A campaign ensures retention, referrals and revenue. You have to give your customers a reason to get excited. And it has to be more than a discount or sale.

Sales are getting to be blasé. JCPenney® stores have discovered that their customers want value everyday, not the hype of another weekend markdown that is supposedly even better than last weekend's markdowns.

Put your marketing team together and come up with four campaigns that you can repeat each year, with a few tweaks to keep them fresh. You can use the seasons, holidays, and piggyback on local events. You can build campaigns around new movies, books, or other celebrity or social news. Partner up with a local charity and help them with their current campaigns. Enter local contests to be the best in our city.

One of our favorites campaigns is to celebrate milestones.

We threw an event when we switched over from Internet to the AM dial and ran a press release along with our other marketing channels.

We campaigned to celebrate our 1000th broadcast, and on the 4th day of each month, we host a *Share 4 Business* Campaign, to help us reach one million listeners.

So often, your company reaches important milestones, yet, you don't share the accomplishment with your customers. These celebrations are built-in trust builders and they increase your credibility and stability in your customer's mind. This is one way to prove to them what a fantastic company you are to work with, and another reason for them to tell others about you.

10 Marketing Channels

10 Marketing Channels

Bonus To Our Readers

We'd like to invite you to be interviewed on The Experience Pros Radio Show.

We're looking for industry experts to share advice on marketing, employee retention, customer service, social media, start-ups, exit strategies, and all topics that a business owner, commission-sales, network marketer or entrepreneur would need to help their thriving company grow.

Fill out the Interview Request Form at www.ExperiencePros.com to be added to the program.

Tune in daily at www.ExperiencePros.com or download the App for podcasts and live streaming.

If you're invited to be on a radio program, use all 10 of your marketing channels to share the campaign. Don't be the world's best-kept secret, become a household name that everyone is talking about.

Chapter 5
Make The Sale

The concepts of marketing seem to baffle many business owners, however, once you create a system with four campaigns per year, you'll discover that the next roadblock to growing your business quickly is found in the sales process, or lack thereof.

In the glory days, you could stand behind your cash register, and the customers would buy. You'd boast a sale, and they'd come flocking in, bringing friends, carelessly adding to their credit card debt. Today, consumers are cautious and bombarded. They are busier than ever. Look around and right now everyone around you is multi-tasking. They're all keeping track of multiple calendars, checking in on FourSquare®, Tweeting, booking virtual meetings, attending a webinar and drinking a protein shake for lunch, all while sitting in the car in between meetings.

Your company is trying to not only grab their attention, they're word-of-mouth referrals, but also their dollars. The orthodontist, photographer and local charity are all competing for those same dollars. Your competition is far more reaching than the other companies in your industry; it's everyone. And everything is available to your customer online with the click of a button.

Consider the steps of your own sales process and compare them to the ease of doing business elsewhere. Your customer is not only shopping around based on price, they're comparing reviews and choosing based on convenience, ease of purchase, and testimonials from their friends and who makes them feel better.

It's not logic that dictates the purchase, so you won't out-logic them with facts, figures and data. You have to win them over with emotion, feeling good and being able to brag about their purchase online.

Your customers are checking in, therefore, telling all their friends about you with one click on their smart phone. If you make this process difficult, their time is too valuable to waste on trying to work it out.

The Sales Process Trifecta

If you have a brick & mortar location, you have one clear place for point-of-sale transactions. But even then, are you still asking your customers to stand in line? Is there a better way that's also quicker? You bet there is, and the sooner you eliminate the phrase "this is how we've always done it" from your vocabulary, the sooner you'll get to the excitement of brainstorming for better ways to serve your customers.

Website | Mobile App | Social Media

Everyday, new options are being brought online to help you help your customers. Long gone are the credit card machines with the duplicate carbon paper where you wrote down the information and scraped your knuckles when swiping with that bulky machine.

While technology is improving every single day, the basics to bringing customers through your sales process still remain the fundamental basis for bringing in revenue.

A simple flow chart will put your sales team at ease by creating a duplicable sales process. This means that every customer, every time, has a consistent experience, that no matter who is at the helm taking caring of the customer, the process remains basically the same.

At each interaction, there is a predictable next step. Each step brings your customer through your sales process, and back again for repeat purchases.

I'm still waiting for the day when the Franklin Covey Company releases the Franklin Planner App. In my head, I imagine the app to have tabs along the side, and the pages to duplicate what they've been printing for years. Much like an e-book, I'll be able to turn the page, swipe the tab, and enter all the information I used to keep all in on place, now all on the mobile app. I've got it all pictured in my head.

Your customers are the key to keeping your technology updated. They can tell you the ideas they have, the reasons they shop with other retailers and the simple way that their favorite online store connects with them, in a very personal way. Don't assume that just because you're new, and because your customers like you, that's enough to keep them loyal. You're competing with too many other vendors to be so naïve.

Many franchises and multi-level marketing companies are tapping into the online resources and more often than not, when you dig deep into what they're offering their customers, it's equated to a highly efficient database system, or online appointment setting, and features that cater to their mobile clients. The product is simply the catalyst.

The founder of the Starbucks® coined the phrase, "We're not in the coffee business, serving people. We're in the people business serving coffee." That means that no matter what industry you're in, you're in the people business.

I read that if radio were invented today, it would be all the rage because of how easily the media interfaces with the on-the-go consumer. You can listen in your car, on your smartphone, at your desk. No matter where you are, you can listen to a radio station in any city or state, thanks to online streaming features and podcasting that's available. You can listen to the radio while doing other things such as driving, working in the yard, catching up on filing and data entry.

No other media can offer that. Television and magazines are limited to having your eyes on the screen, yet radio is far more visual because the listener fills in the images for themselves, therefore, making it so personal to the end listener. It's the Visa® of media.

Your company has the ability to be the Visa® of your industry.

Stop trying to create another brochure for your business. Instead, create another point of sale to make it easier for your customer to do business with you.

Start considering every point of entry, not as a brochure for your company, but as platform for creating new business. Each point of entry can be a place to create a transaction.

Your business card can be used to create a sale, in exchange for a free cup of coffee, a discount, or an added gift with purchase. Most business cards find their way into the trash because they have no value to them. Unless someone is trying to build up his or her database with new entries, your contact information isn't worth saving when I can easily look you up online.

Your website has multiple opportunities for creating passive revenue streams. Check out some of your favorites from a vendor point of view, and you'll start to see the possibilities.

Besides your main product or service, you can offer pdf downloads, promotional products with your logo and tag line, eBooks, webinars, and how-to videos. You can repackage your products to create a new offer. Most likely, you already have the content and the resources in-house.

The more interactive your website is, the more interesting it is to visit and to invite others to visit. Your website is not a brochure. It's your interactive virtual store.

Your e-book is not a brochure, but a gateway to new business. Include QR (Quick Response) codes that take your reader to a landing page to download updates and new content.

We interact heavily on our Facebook page during our live broadcasts, so we encourage our listeners to visit our social media page.

The Experience Pros Facebook Page QR Code

Once someone has a copy of your book, and they're reading it, you obviously have their attention, but only for the moment. That moment will pass far to soon if you're not intentional about building your company. Weave the benefits of doing business with your company into the e-book and include a special promotion that is unique to your reader. In 2012, e-book downloads are expected to reach $3 billion dollars in sales. How much of the pie would you like to participate in? But the end goal is not selling a book, or adding new fans to your pages, its bringing new customers through your sales process.

When you host an event, such as a Ribbon Cutting, the end goal is not fill the room with a crowd. The purpose is to introduce prospects to your company and bring them through your sales process. Most companies open the doors and expect the customers to take the next step. Too often, a vendor will host an event and complain a few months later that they didn't get any new business from it. Really? What did you do to create any new business?

You need to create a call-to-action at the event.

You need to follow up afterwards.

During the event, you need to showcase your benefits rather than expecting the tray of cheese and crackers to do it for you.

You need to send your guests off with a token that brings them back to you and creates a sense of urgency.

All the marketing in the world will ensure that people have heard of you and bring them *to* your sales process. It's up to you to take them *through* your sales process.

Without customers, you don't have a multi-million dollar business, you have an expensive hobby.

Chapter 6
Retain Your Customers

Every interaction with your customer is the gateway to the next interaction with your customer. The courting of a new customer is fairly expected and built in. You'll call. You'll email. You'll drop off samples and present them with raving testimonials. You pretty much turn over every loose stone to get them to buy from you. But after the sale, this is where extreme customer service needs to kick in.

Your customer doesn't expect to hear from you again until you're in a crunch or having a promotion and you need them to "Buy Now". All of a sudden, it's an emergency to get them to purchase. Don't miss out! Today Only! Freak out your customer and back them into an impulse purchase!

Yes, this can be a viable business option, but it's not sustainable. You aren't after satisfied customers, you want loyal customers who shop with you regularly and invite their friends to do the same. The number one proven method for increasing sales and retaining customers is having a consistent follow up strategy.

The number one proven system that is missing in struggling companies is the lack of a consistent follow up strategy.

If you follow up with your customers, they will think of you more often. If you follow up with your customers, they will shop with you more often. If you follow up with your customers, they will tell others about you, and they do it more often.

The average company brings in 30% more customers every year, yet they lose 30% of their customer base out the back door due to lack of a retention strategy.

They never hear from you. Or worse, the only time they hear from you is when you want them to open up their checkbook (or virtually swipe their card). That's not a relationship, that's a transaction.

The very best flyer to send to your customers isn't a postcard, though I really like postcards. Postcards are an ideal flyer to send to prospect and current customers, if they include a reason to hold on to it, such as helpful tips or a sporting calendar, they will be tacked up on a bulletin board for all the world to see. If it's simply an oversized business card, don't waste your money. It will get pitched in the recycling bin faster than you can say print-your-own-postage.

Take the time to make it valuable. Include a gift with purchase, or a special incentive. Add a checklist of the *7 Top Ways To Improve Their Situation or Solve Their Pain* – and be sure that it ties directly to your brand.

The very best flyer to send to your customers isn't a coupon, though coupons can create a sense of urgency getting your customers back in the door again.

If you're going to slash your prices, make it worthwhile for everyone, including your time and energy to print and promote. 15% off rarely creates frenzy out the door. $100.00 off will stir the crowd, but you need to stay in business.

Every grocery chain in town offers a weekly "loss leader" in order to drive customers into the store. They entice you with 99 cents a pound for a lobster, in hopes that while you're there, you'll stock up on other essentials, too. Without the bonus of the deal, you may shop somewhere else, or not at all.

You can duplicate a "Loss Leader" with your own campaigns, as long as you have other items that your customers might also like, *as long as they're there.*

The very best promotional item you can mail to your customer to strengthen your relationship with them, and to keep your brand top-of-mind, is a handwritten note card. Not an e-card. Not a post card, and never, never undo the sentiment by including the words "By the way, I'd appreciate your referrals."

A handwritten note card doesn't require a special occasion.

A handwritten note card can be written for no reason at all, other than, "I really appreciate you and I'm grateful that you bring your business to me." You don't need to wait for a campaign, you can write one today.

Handwritten notecards are often the first item opened when filtering through a stack of mail. Handwritten note cards are often displayed. Handwritten note cards are shared. Handwritten note cards are saved.

Handwritten notecards are the best value you can invest in to connect with your customers.

Your business is made up of people. Your business is made up of people with busy lives, hopes and dreams. Everyday, they struggle with challenges, just like you do.

The world can be a mean, dark and ugly place. Everyday we battle with strangers on the highway and people who criticize and complain. Bad news and gossip travel too easily and infiltrate well-meaning companies and families. The antidote to all that is angry and dark in the world is to share kindness.

We say that Kindness Is So Simple, and everyday we encourage our listeners to give someone a 20-second K.I.S.S. Your smile, holding a door open, saying thank you and every day, looking at your database and being truly grateful for all that you've been given, is the act that will change your mindset into growing a multi-million dollar enterprise.

Business is not rocket-science, it's people science. Your company has the foundation for being a multi-million-dollar enterprise, but only if you treat it that way. Give it the attention it deserves and the rewards will far outweigh the sacrifices.

Put what's truly important into your calendar. Take time each day to appreciate all that you've been given and take advantage of the time you have.

Live well. Live the life you dream of living.

Laugh much. Find joy in the small things. Appreciate life for its laughter.

Love much. Love makes the world go round. When you love what you do, who you spend your time with, you'll find that time is what you make it to be.

Send Handwritten Cards Everyday

The Experience Pros Radio Show

Together, Angel Tuccy and Eric Reamer are the hosts of The Experience Pros Radio Show, named The Most Positive Business Talk Show in America. They are the founders of Experience Pros University, co-authors of Lists That Saved My Business, Leading The Revolution, the creators of the audio seminar SUPER-Marketing.

They started an Internet Radio Show in 2009. Within 6months, the show switched to the AM dial. In a 15-month time frame, they grew the program to 5 stations across the country, and expanded into a 2-hour daily talk show featuring experts from all across the world. The show is unique because it features the best in business and the positive impact that entrepreneurs and small business has on the American economy.

Fan Braggin'™ is The Experience Pros signature trademark, and every Friday, they open up the phone lines to callers bragging about good customer service. Callers taking the time to say something nice about somebody else in business are rewarded with a few minutes of free PR for their own companies.

You can't call and tell Eric and Angel that your company offers great customer service until first, you tell say something nice about somebody else. The branding is consistent all the way down to the phone number 1-855-FAN-BRAG.

About The Authors

Angel Tuccy was named 2011 Inspirational Leader of the Year by the SMDCC Women In Leadership organization, and the 2012 Hall of Fame Winner for the Highlands Ranch Chamber. Angel is the best selling author of Lists That Saved My Life. She loves to write, read and travel with her family. She sits on the board of directors for the Chamber of Commerce of Highlands Ranch and runs a professional women's group called Ladies Who Lunch. Angel and her husband, Jay are the parents of three teenagers. They live in Denver, Colorado.

Eric Reamer has served in a management capacity for numerous companies, restaurants and non-profit organizations over the course of twenty-five years. He traveled across the United States and internationally as a public speaker and professional stage illusionist. He enjoys reading and writing, and anything having to do with coffee. Eric has been a professional-level member of the National Speakers Association, and loves training others how to communicate their message more dynamically. Eric is the father of two sons, and lives in Denver, Colorado.

Find out more about Eric and Angel at
www.ExperiencePros.com.

Experience Pros Radio Show
The Most Positive Business Talk Show In America
Inspiring You to Get Your Business Right

The Experience Pros Radio Show is your daily in-your-pocket, in-the-car, in-your-office, business training.

- Broadcast live Monday through Friday, in Denver. Look up your local listings for times. Stream at www.ExperiencePros.com.

- Participate in live chat and online conversation during the show on www.Facebook.com/ExperiencePros

- Download podcasts on from the Experience Pros Radio Show App, iTunes or on ExperiencePros.com

Call 1-855-FAN-BRAG to talk about great customer service.

What are you waiting for?
Share the Revolution!
www.ExperiencePros.com

"I am totally addicted to the Experience Pros radio show! Thank you for adding value to my day and to my life!" - Rachel Lyman, Denver Metro Chamber of Commerce

"Experience Pros has one of the most engaged and motivated listening audiences." - Ely Delaney, owner of Your Marketing University

"Angel and Eric are very kind and gracious hosts. Thank you so much for having me as a regular guest on your show. You truly are the most positive business talk show." - Bob Burg, Author of the Go-Giver

"The Experience Pros Radio show is one of the most positive radio shows. I have learned so much from Eric and Angel... how to prospect, how to "filter" my customers and business and how to network socially." - Cheryl Braunschweiger, ALMC Mortgage

"Experience Pros is all about treating others with respect, understanding, being positive and listening. You live what you do and I just want to say Thank you and continue the revolution!" – Cristin Tarr, Business Service Corps

"Eric and Angel host the most positive business talk show in America." – Dr. Ivan Misner, Founder of BNI Worldwide Networking Group

"I listen to your show from Australia. I really like the pro-active approach that Experience Pros takes for the small business entrepreneur. No one else seems to focusing on helping small business." Michael Russo, Why Bankruptcy Rocks

Lists That Saved My Business
Eliminate Cold Calling with Relationship Marketing

Lists That Saved My Business is the compelling story of Angel Tuccy and Eric Reamer and how they found success for their company, Experience Pros, LLC.

Angel and Eric will help you create a revolution in the way people treat people in business, starting today... with the customers you already have!

- Eliminate cold-calls
- Drive more people to your sales process
- Increase customer retention

Lists That Saved My Business is the perfect tool for business owners, sales managers and marketing experts. You'll find yourself referring back to this book again and again.

What are you waiting for?
Share the Revolution!
www.ExperiencePros.com

Not sure why, but I seem to be getting more out of this book the second time through. Make sure to keep this book handy if you own a business. Love the checklists at the end of the chapters! – Connie Ellefson

Angel and Eric have created a book that is a "must have" for every business library. Lists that Saved My Business is an easy, comprehensive book that outlines all the basics of building business relationships that need to be in place in order to make you stand out set you apart in the market. The lists that Angel and Eric have put together at the end of each chapter are a great recap with thought provoking goals and action steps to get your business growing. This is an excellent reference book that you will want to keep close and refer to often! – Gina Kaelin-Westcott

If you intend to succeed in your business, you need to act with deliberate purpose. You need to plan your work and work your plan. You've heard it all before. What you haven't heard is HOW this kind of forethought can achieve amazing results. Angel and Eric, The Experience Pros prove how revolutionary a systematic, deliberate, positive action plan can be used to not only satisfy your customers, but astound them. – Robert Spalding

The ideas are in bite-sized pieces and the book reads fast. I will be changing my business card processing after networking events. Ping and purge. What I like the most is the emphasis on building relationships with people. It's natural for me to do so sometimes I do not utilize the entire value of that innate skill. And once I begin a business relationship what the hay do I do with it? The book handles that in so many ways. – David Veal

SUPER-Marketing
Audio Seminar

The How-To Course on Generating
Word-of-Mouth Marketing that Out-Performs
Your Own Efforts!

This 60-minute audio seminar will teach you:

- Quick and easy ways to market your business

- Healthy business alternatives to marketing

- Common mistakes to avoid

- Where to get the best return on your marketing dollars

SUPER-Marketing is the time-tested, proven-effective system of generating word-of-mouth buzz. Your marketing answers can all be found in the four major sections of the grocery store, and your guides will point out each of the items that you SHOULD be doing... and what items you need to put a FREEZE on!

What are you waiting for?
Share the Revolution!
www.ExperiencePros.com

Ben Franklin said, "If a man empties his purse into his head, no one can take it away from him. An investment in knowledge always pays the best interest."

The moment I saw a new product with the names Angel Tuccy and Eric Reamer associated with it, I knew it was a MUST HAVE.

With the investment of very few dollars and only an hour of your time, this audio program will take some of the very things you probably do each day and transform them into customer/client referral marketing machines.

They take the listener through seven steps that will turn such things as e-mail signatures, referral rewards, and networking events into an on-going and residual word of mouth marketing plan. For example, the strategy they discuss about when to reward someone for a referral is so simple and sensible that it will have you slapping your forehead saying, "Of course that's how to do it!" It'll even save you some money in the long run.

The analogy of the grocery store tour as you take the steps is brilliant! I can tell you, I won't be spending time in the frozen food aisle anymore than absolutely necessary - listen to this CD and you'll know why - Hey, it's cold in there!

I first listened in my car to and from the office and then immediately took it inside and listened again with pen to paper. These are strategies that are now incorporated in my 2011 overall success plan! – Mark Crowley

Lists That Saved My Life

As a perpetual list-maker and working mom, Angel Tuccy, shares her secrets for balancing family, career and her personal life.

Angel shares her everyday trials of raising a family while running a corporation and turns it all into manageable checklists that ensure everything gets done, including finding personal time for herself.

Gain valuable insight and helpful tips on:

- Time-Saving Tips
- Increasing Your Budget
- Running A Smooth Happy Household
- Setting Family Goals
- Gaining Help From Your Family

…And getting all those daily details under control!

Lists That Saved My Life is the very tool all working moms have been waiting for.

What are you waiting for? Share the Revolution!
www.ExperiencePros.com

I recommend that you pick up Angel's book, Lists That Saved My Life. The entire book is a master's level course in event management told in story form. There's not a single thing in the stories that we can't relate to at a certain level - some of it deeply. – Mark Crowley, KNUS/KRKS Radio

Angel is a remarkable speaker, trainer and an accomplished author. Her ability to connect with others truly inspires all who come in contact with her to listen to what this exceptional person has to say in regard to the "Extreme Customer Service" skills she, and her partner Eric Reamer, teach. She unquestionably inspires you to strive for your best as she touches you with her truly angelic nature. Any organization would be wise to connect with Angel and Eric, to learn the "Extreme Customer Service" skills they teach. – Rob Hale, Travel-N-Relax

Lists That Saved My Life is an easy read that everyone should pick up. This book helps you realize which lists are most important, how to organize your busy life, and still manage a good balance of work and family. You will find this book to be very conversational. Angel speaks right to you, and provides tons of amazing insight. – Lindsay Hernandez, BWT Risk Advisor

Bonus Chapter Excerpt from
Lists That Saved My Business

In a market full of overwhelming choices, competitive prices and message overload, it seems that businesses are finding it more and more difficult to connect with customers in a new and fresh way. Is bigger and faster always better? In a rushed society, sometimes we forget to slow down and realize that our customers are real people, just like us.

When you stop and take a deep breath, you'll be able to hear the heartbeat of your business: it's your customers. When you spend some time actually listening to your customers, focusing on the people and not just the sale, you can connect and create a loyal customer base that brags about your service. The key to extreme customer service is old-fashioned really; stay in touch with your customers.

Pauline Szafranski, the vice president of marketing for Lotus Concepts agrees that business is going back to a grassroots mentality. "Everything was over-the-top, big and impersonal for a decade," says Szafranski. "The backlash has made people pick up the phone instead of emailing, write thank you notes, and take time for a business lunch instead of faxing over contracts."

Today's consumers don't want to be bombarded with sales pitches. They want to feel valued and important. Finding a way to reach your customers without interrupting them or intruding on them will help them feel like they are participants, rather than being manipulated into a purchase.

To help you stay in touch with your customers, we put together nine protocols that will connect you with them, create extreme customer service and release loyal ambassadors for your brand into the world.

#1 – Email

Email is the most crowded and overused, but also the most expected form of communication. So if you're going to send an email, make it personal and *never* send spam or junk mail.

Always ask permission to place someone on your newsletter mailing list. If you don't know the person well enough to pick up the phone and call them, they don't belong on your list. If it's someone you know, who knows you, or has an inkling of interest, then you're probably okay, but we would still recommend asking. If your relationship is too weak to ask, then you are at risk to losing them to your competition.

There's a reason consumers call it "junk" mail. Don't send junk. Ever. Use email to send a personal note and share information.

TIPS FOR SENDING EFFECTIVE EMAILS

Always include your contact information and logo in your email signature. If you send something worthwhile, the hope is that your message will be forwarded. Make sure people can contact you.

Do not use email to make a decision or conduct a conversation; too much is left up to interpretation.

Keep the subject line of your email current with the discussion thread. Change the subject box, for example, if the conversation has moved away from the conference that is taking place next week to the promotional products for the next trade show.

Be clear about whether or not you expect a reply.

#2 - Telephone

The telephone, which can sometimes be viewed as weighing 100 pounds, is one of your greatest links to building rapport. In the age of quick emails, the phone can be a welcome channel for making solid connections. If you need a quick response, the telephone can often be quicker than email.

There are times when you need to make sales calls, but we like to think of your telephone more as an additional way to connect with your customers. Don't always use the telephone to make a sales pitch. Sometimes, your customers just need to hear your voice. These conversations can often take on a life of their own and when you listen intently, you might just learn something that helps you help them.

Tips for Leaving Effective Phone Messages

Leave a brief, yet clear message with your name and phone number, even if you're sure they have caller ID. Tell the recipient who you are, why you are calling, and how to respond. We've had phone messages where the name of the caller was fuzzy and we didn't recognize the number. These phone calls don't get returned quickly – if at all.

Keep your messages brief. Think about what you want to say before you dial. More often than not, you will be sent to voicemail, so be prepared to leave a short message, not your entire sales pitch.

Leave your phone number at the beginning and at the end of the phone message.

Avoid leaving this message: "Hi, it's me. Call me back." Unless you are calling your very best golfing buddy, who knows exactly why you are calling because you have been best friends since the third grade... this is *not* an effective phone message.

Use your own answering message to create a memory. We already know you that you can't take our call right now, because we got your voicemail. So use your message to bring a smile to my face instead. We call it "disrupting their complacency." If you can keep your customers out of "voice message coma", you can get them to talk about your voicemail message and even get others to call you and keep sharing it. Let your next caller feel compelled to tell two friends...and so on, and so on.

Here's a great example: *"Do you hear that sizzle? Can you smell that aroma? I'm in the kitchen cooking up something delectable for lunch today. Place your catering order and I'll cook lunch for you tomorrow."*

Keep your answering message short, but professionally interesting.

Return phone messages. Call your customers back every time they call you... preferably before the close of the business day.

#3 – U.S. Mail

Sending a handwritten letter, card or note can go a long way in creating long-term customers, and offering extreme customer service. You can almost guarantee that your handwritten card will be opened, especially if it's personal. Handwritten cards never lose their luster, and a personalized note can make a powerful and positive impact on your customer.

We keep a memo board of the cards we receive, and it's about time for a second board! Sometimes the best pick-me-up on a rough day is to read a friendly note from someone who took time out of his or her busy day to say, "You matter". We all struggle everyday, and a genuine note can really mean a lot. It only takes you a few minutes, but the impact is far greater. If you need some tips on what to say, visit a greeting card website or ExperiencePros.com for starters. If you write something genuine and heartfelt, it will be right.

Tips for Writing Cards

Make it personal and hand-written.

Include your logo on the envelope or stamp.

Remember birthday cards, anniversary cards, get well cards, thank you cards and notes of appreciation.

When the postmaster raises prices, send your customers a page of 2-cent stamps.

Send cards every day to people you meet and always send a thank you after the sale.

Cards are often shared and displayed for others to take notice, whereas a note on letterhead is typically filed or even tossed.

#4 - Face-to-Face

When your customer is involved in the buying process, you are focused on offering great customer service. But, what are you doing for them *after* the sale or before they've decided to purchase again? A client doesn't care how much you know until they know how much you care.

Tips for Face-to-Face Interaction

Drop in and visit in between appointments or when you happen to be in the area. This gesture goes a long way in creating a genuine customer connection. Bringing treats ensures that the office staff looks forward to your "drop-in".

Set up a coffee date. We like to hold what we call, "non-dinner dinner parties". Like many people in business, we found that coffee meetings were well suited to our business, and allowed an opportunity for us to get to know others, as well as them to get to know us. We also discovered that having five or six coffee meetings each week was really eating into our available time.

In an effort to replicate the value of a dinner party where twelve to fourteen guests get together to meet one another, we decided to host "non-dinner dinner parties" and we set them up like this: Each week we schedule a time to meet someone for coffee. This could be a current client, a potential client, or someone we're just starting to get to know. Leading up that coffee date, when we receive other invitations for coffee, we add them to the existing coffee meeting. The result is five or six people having coffee together. The meetings are very dynamic. In many cases these people might never otherwise meet, and the outcome is refreshing. If you don't have a lot of time to set up three to five coffee meetings per week, the "non-dinner dinner party" is just for you.

Give them leads. Referrals from you are a great way to add intrinsic value in your customer's mind. Giving leads to your customers keeps you on the top of their list of people to call, and that's always a good thing. You might just discover that goodwill is reciprocal.

Ask them how you can serve them better. Rather than sending a generic survey that doesn't really give you the answers you're looking for, ask the real questions face-to-face. More than their words, you'll get a truer response from their facial expressions and body language. If you can help your customer to know that you're listening, you can make real changes that will impact them immediately – and that level of concern will help keep you on the top of their list of quality people doing quality business.

> Create a conversation and ask your customers, "What do you want me to KEEP doing, to STOP doing or to START doing?" Then listen and respond appropriately. Spend time talking with your customers about how you can serve them better, and ask them why they chose you over someone else.

Meeting with your customers face-to-face will help you learn more about their needs, create conversation and bring out solutions. Customers respond favorably when you care enough to spend some time with them. To create extreme customer service, you must care about your customers as people.

Memories are built face-to-face. If you're going to offer extreme customer service, you have to create a memory for your customer to talk about. You need to convert the buying process into a memorable experience. Do something for your customers that they can't expect anywhere else. The goal is to get your customers to brag about you.

Your customers will rarely be more excited about your brand than you are, so you need to be positively contagious and enthusiastic.

#5 - INVITATIONS

Inviting your customers to an event is a great way to re-connect. If it's been a while since they've seen you, heard from you, or purchased from you, invite them to an event and you can rekindle that connection.

Tips for Using Invitations to Stay In Touch

Plan an event of your own, or invite customers to an event that is already happening. Take advantage of the events your community puts together and never go anywhere with your passenger seat empty. Always invite and take along a customer or two.

An invitation is a non-threatening approach to building extreme customer service. It's also a great way to create a dialogue with potential customers.

Match your own passion and be creative. Invite your customers to something you enjoy – and better yet – something you know they enjoy, too. Sporting, cultural, and civic events are going on in your town every week. Check out your local trade magazine or newspaper and plan ahead.

An even better way to get customers through your door and in front of your brand is to create your own gala. Celebrate a milestone, host a fundraiser, or make up any excuse to pull people together. Mix and Mingle Mondays, Trendy Tuesdays, and Wake-Up Wednesdays are creative places to start. Look at the upcoming movies and host a pre-show party. Throw a celebration for the hot trends happening in your industry, and you'll have a never-ending supply of reasons to pull people together.

If you haven't had a ribbon cutting or milestone celebration this year, join your local chamber of commerce and get on their calendar. This is a great way to announce your presence in your community, even if you've already been in business for eight years.

Make the presentation as special as you can. You don't have to spend a lot of money, but you do have to spend some time planning out the details and inviting your guests to show up. Invitations, balloons, door prizes and refreshments that show off your theme or color scheme can turn a ho-hum month into a line of people that are reminded of your brand and who want to do business with you.

Secure the event in your customer's memory with a memento of the occasion. Just like souvenirs or vacation photos, a promotional item that complements the occasion will trigger your customer's memory of you long after the event is over.

Spend time doing what you enjoy with people that you enjoy. You will create very loyal customers when you spend time together. If you are hosting an event, incorporate others to help with the work so that you can spend time mingling with your guests. You will discover many stories that will strengthen your customer relationships.

#6 – Follow-Through

Every customer interaction is an opportunity to re-engage your customer in conversation or bring them further into your sales process. Once you develop a strategic follow-through plan that is automatic and consistent, you will see an increase in sales and customer interaction that is brought forward by your customer, rather than by you. Lost sales are hinged on the lack of follow-through in your planning. Much like your golf swing or tennis serve, the ball goes farther when you follow through. Too often, sales grow cold and money is left on the table when you fail to follow-through with your customers.

Tips for an Effective Follow-Through Plan

Follow up every conversation, email, or newsletter. There should be a constant conversation that is developed through your automatic follow through system. Just as an example: Each conversation should be followed through with an email. Each email response should be followed through with another email or perhaps, a phone call. Each newsletter should be followed through with a phone call or a post card.

When you have an automatic plan for response, you'll never have to wonder if your clients have fallen through the proverbial cracks of being too busy to follow-through. Sure, it takes time, but what else are you doing that is more important than taking care of your customers? The plus side of all of this is that once you have a system in place, you can delegate it and outsource it, because you will be adding new staff to help take care of the customers.

Automatic is not the same as "automated". With an automatic system, you automatically know what step comes next and you personally follow through. You never have to answer for, or make excuses for a real person reaching out to connect with your customers. On the other end of the spectrum, "automated" refers to having a computer-generated follow-through system that isn't personal, and that often ends up causing more frustration for the customers. This causes frustration for your staff as well, for having to answer the question, "Why can't I get a real person to help me?"

When you keep in touch with your customers, they remember to do business with you *and* they tell others to do the same. The key is to stay on their mind, and a satisfactory sales experience will *not* do the trick. Satisfied customers shop around. Satisfied customers are easily swayed away by the competition, referrals from their own friends, or convenience. Unless you keep your brand fresh in your customer's memory, someone else will reap the next purchase.

> Don't let neglect be the reason your customers shop around. Be consistent. Let your customers hear from you all year long, not just when its time to purchase.

Here is a great way to follow through with that customer who was shopping around but purchased somewhere else: Send them a handwritten note card thanking them for the opportunity to offer them a price quote. Most likely, the company they chose didn't even thank them for their business, and here you are with a note card with a handwritten sentiment that says you care and that you hope they were well served.

Who do you think they will talk about? YOU! Who do you think will get their referral business, even though they didn't purchase from you? YOU! Who do you think they will turn to when things go awry and they need help fast? It will be you! Following through builds your business in ways that nothing else will.

#7 - REWARDS

Give your customers something they weren't expecting. Reward your customers just for sharing your name. This is a behavior that you want your customers to repeat over and over again; so rewarding them for doing it is a really good idea. It's exciting when someone sends you a lead. You can encourage them to do it again and again with a little bit of behavioral reinforcement – but not in a typical "referral program" sort of way.

Tips for Rewarding your Customers

A typical "referral program" is when you reward the referring party *after* a transaction has taken place with a bonus of some sort. On the surface, this seems like a good idea. Maybe you've been the recipient of such a referral program or you've read about other companies who offer something similar.

If you pay someone for referring a customer to you once the transaction is over, that qualifies as a "commission", not as a referral reward. Your new customer may begin to wonder if the referral was genuine, or did they just get sucked-in to help make someone a little cash on the side.

It is not up to your customers to make the sale for you – that's *your* job. You simply want them to send potential customers your way. Whether or not they actually purchase is irrelevant when paying out a true referral reward.

You want to reward the behavior of the referral; "Tell people about me. Make an introduction, and help me get the word out that I exist."

Instead of paying out a $50.00 bonus once a transaction has occurred, try taking that same $50.00 and invest in ten $5.00 gifts. These can be coffee mugs with your logo, specialty items that match your branding, movie tickets or gift cards to the local coffee shop.

Now, instead of paying out one commission for one referral, you get to pay out ten times. Watch how much quicker your referrals come in! We like to hand out gift cards anytime someone introduces us to someone new. These are people we might not have otherwise met, and they are being brought to us with a glowing introduction. We definitely want to reward that!

Whether or not a sale ever takes place is up to us, and is determined by the timing and needs of the new contact. But no matter what, we want to reward the introduction, so we hand out gift cards (we often keep one or two with us) or we send them in the mail along with a handwritten thank you card.

#8 – REPEAT RECEIPTS

Rewarding your existing customers has an overwhelmingly positive impact on both your customers *and* your team. Everyone gets in on the fun and excitement – and the energy creates a buzz for your brand.   Repeat Reccipts can do that for you.

Tips for Repeat Receipts

Target your existing customers – at the cash register, at the door, when they check out.

Hand out rewards to entice them to come back the very next day or the very next week. Encourage the behavior you're after. You want them to return quickly and be so excited that they tell other people about it.

Use what you've already got. The little plastic pizza piece that keeps the cheese from sticking to the pizza box can be redeemed the next day for a smoking' hot deal. Michael's prints a 40% off coupon on their cash-register receipts. Kohl's gives you a $10.00 voucher for every $50 spent.

Never let your customer leave without an enticement to get them right back. Otherwise, when do you plan to see them again? Put a date on it.

#9 – Advertise

You've heard of Coke and Pepsi. You could knock on one hundred doors and find out that everyone has heard of these companies. You've heard of State Farm Insurance, Chase Bank, and Oprah Winfrey.

You've heard of them because you keep seeing them on television, reading about them in newspapers and seeing their ads in magazines.

Companies that advertise become familiar to their audience. Familiarity creates a sense of credibility and trust. Advertising warms your marketing and sales efforts. It doesn't replace word-of-mouth marketing; it compliments it. Advertising is a way to leverage your efforts so your customers see your brand, even when you're not there.

Pete Blackshaw says that the radio and television ads that reap the highest attention are for brands with great website strategies along with their advertising. "Doritos, Federal Express, Budweiser, GoDaddy® and every major television and cable network have integrated their websites to keep their advertising more engaging."

Pepsi® ran an experiment where they dropped their television ads in the Super Bowl to focus on Internet advertising and social media. Blackshaw suggests that companies can't afford to abandon advertising on radio and television completely.

Pepsi® didn't stop all of their television advertising; but they *enhanced* it by doing something different and then tying that change to another form of marketing.

TIPS FOR ADVERTISING

Start with your FRANC™ circle. (Friends, Relatives, Associates, Neighbors/Networks & Customers) Who do you know that produces a magazine, or has connections for radio advertising? Does your trade association offer advertising to your favorite customers? Most national companies that advertise on the radio are based in the hometown of the radio personalities that they started with. Start with whom you know.

Focus on reaching your favorite customers. You can ask your current customers to help create your ads. You can run a contest as a great campaign, and you'll have several options to choose from.

Advertising isn't just for television. Consider magazines, radio, billboards, and community events. Let your current customers know about your ads and where to find them. They'll feel like they've chosen the right company because you're obviously going to be around to take care of them for a while.

Use the Internet. It's where so many eyes are. Don't underestimate the power of Internet advertising. A company that makes cupcake stands started with Internet advertising and created a quarter-million dollar company in their first year.

Post your ads on your website. Include extras like outtakes, bloopers and extended versions. Customers like to feel as if they know a secret, so include behind-the-scenes pieces and scarcely known trivia.

Blog about your ads. Include links to find your ad. Make it easy for browsers to share your ad with others with the click of a button.

Blackshaw shares the story of how even major advertisers can sometimes forget to focus on their customers. "When General Motors wanted to create their new advertisement for the Chevy Tahoe, they partnered with *The Apprentice* television show. GM encouraged the show's participants to create their own television ads. While this campaign gained a lot of media attention, it didn't translate into customer loyalty, or even a boost in sales.

GM missed the number one rule in advertising. The contest wasn't focused on their target market: Chevy Tahoe drivers. Most of the ads created were by people who had never purchased or even driven the cars. As a result, the ads lacked the genuine passion and enthusiasm that sends customers running into dealerships."

Focus on speaking to your favorite customers and don't quit too soon. Often, when people start advertising, they expect an immediate return on their investment. In most cases, it takes some time to create trust and familiarity before a customer will buy-in to your brand. They are learning about you, and getting to know you.

When we started our radio show, we thought that our advertisement for Experience Pros University would fill a new class every week. It was professionally produced with Angel's voice and a beautiful musical background. We didn't get our first new student from that ad until six months after it started running. The temptation was strong to pull the ad and say, "it didn't work". It does work. Especially when it's combined with other methods of marketing. General Douglas MacArthur says, "Quitting wrinkles the soul." Stay the course. It's worth it.

In business, if you treat customer service as a hobby and don't commit to the daily care and feeding of the heartbeat of your business, then the only heartbeat you will be hearing will be your own.

Your customers are waiting to hear from you. Don't let them down. Your attention may surprise them and they will tell someone about it. If they talked about you once, you can get them to do it again... provided you treat them right.

List for Staying In Touch with Customers

1. Email
2. Telephone
3. U.S. Mail
4. Face-to-Face
5. Invitations
6. Follow Through
7. Reward Referrals
8. Repeat Receipts
9. Advertise

--Read more of *Lists That Saved My Business* by downloading the eBook. --

Also by Angel Tuccy & Eric Reamer

Lists That Saved My Life
(December 2009)

Lists That Saved My Business
(August 2010)

Sex, Drugs & Rock N Roll,
3 Keys For A Healthier Lifestyle
(November 2010)
With Dr. Nick Caras

Leading The Revolution
(December 2010)

SUPER-Marketing - Audio
(December 2010)

Mommy Has Lots To Do
(February 2011)
With Alycia Tuccy

Chase Your Dreams Without
Messing Up Your Manicure
(April 2011)

Lists That Saved My Day
(November 2012)

Website: www.ExperiencePros.com
Blog: www.ExperienceProsBlog.com
Twitter @ExperiencePros
Facebook: Facebook.com/ExperiencePros
Mobile App: Experience Pros Radio Show

www.ingramcontent.com/pod-product-compliance
Lightning Source LLC
Chambersburg PA
CBHW061511180526
45171CB00001B/137